MYS

at Marin Marsh

Denise M. Jordan
Illustrated by Carol Stutz

Rigby®

A Harcourt Achieve Imprint

www.Rigby.com
1-800-531-5015

Literacy by Design Leveled Readers: *Mystery at Marin Marsh*

ISBN-13: 978-1-4189-3919-9
ISBN-10: 1-4189-3919-6

Printed in China
1 2 3 4 5 6 7 8 985 13 12 11 10 09 08 07 06

CONTENTS

DEDICATION

To Mrs. Knox's sixth grade advisory class at Ben Geyer Middle School:

Thank you so much for your criticisms, your suggestions, and most of all, your enthusiasm. You helped me get this project in on deadline.

Thanks also to Bill Horan, Aquatic Specialist at the Wells County Purdue University Extension office. Your expertise was invaluable.

CHAPTER 1

Wetlands or Wastelands?

Mrs. Knox called her sixth-grade science class to attention. "I need to know how each group is going to address how pollution affects our environment."

"Let's do water birds," Nezzie whispered. "I love Canada geese."

"How about the food chain?" suggested Theresa. "What do you think, Robin?"

"I don't want to do any of it," answered Robin. "I hate the marsh. It's full of bugs and weeds."

"Nezzie," said Mrs. Knox, interrupting their conversation, "what's your group's choice?"

"We want to do the marshland food chain," Nezzie said. Theresa nodded. Robin shrugged.

"You have one week. You also have individual oral reports to give. Each of you needs to explain what you gained by doing your project. Now, have a good Labor Day holiday. I'll see you all on Tuesday," Mrs. Knox said.

On the bus, Nezzie and Theresa joined in the conversations around them. Robin watched quietly. She wondered how long it would take her to adjust to a new school and a new family.

Robin's parents had been divorced for two years. Robin was used to that now. Life had actually gotten better after the divorce, although it meant she only saw her mother, who worked as a flight attendant, every once in a while.

This summer, Tom Jones, Robin's dad, had married Jill Anderson, Nezzie's mom. Everything had changed. Jill Anderson was Jill Jones. Robin had a stepmother. Nezzie had a stepfather. And the girls were instant sisters—stepsisters.

Right after the wedding, Robin and her father had moved to Goose Haven Farm, where Nezzie and her mom lived. Her dad and Mama Jill had wanted Robin to get settled before starting at a new school, where her father would be teaching for the first time.

Mama Jill was great, thought Robin. And she and Nezzie were working things out. Nezzie was decent most of the time. It had to be hard for her, too. Nezzie's father, Dr. Jack Anderson, had died in a car accident several years ago.

But right now, she had to focus on this science project. School had hardly started and already she had work to think about. Even worse, she was going to have to talk in front of a bunch of kids she hardly knew!

Early next morning, someone knocked on the door. Robin heard Nezzie scramble down the stairs to the door.

A minute later, Robin's door burst open. "Come on, slowpoke," said Nezzie. "Theresa's here."

"I'm ready," Robin said. She yawned. "Why do we have to go so early?"

Theresa laughed. "If you want to see much in the marsh, you have to go early."

Robin flopped back on her bed. "Well, I don't want to see anything. The marsh is hot and sticky." She plumped her pillow behind her head. "Wake me up when you guys get back."

Nezzie yanked the pillow away. "We've got to start on our project today."

Theresa grabbed one of Robin's hands and Nezzie grabbed the other. "Fine, I'm coming," Robin said.

"What are you girls doing?" Mrs. Jones asked from the doorway.

"We're going to Marin Marsh," answered Nezzie. "We're starting our science project today."

"Oh, yes," Mrs. Jones said. "You girls be careful and remember the rules. And take care of Robin. She didn't grow up around the marsh like you two did."

"I'm not a baby," said Robin. "I don't need them to take care of me."

"It's got nothing to do with being a baby," said Mrs. Jones. "You're not familiar with the marsh."

"I'll do what they say," grumbled Robin.

The girls went downstairs. At once, Nezzie's dog, Smitty, ran to join them. "Let's get going," said Nezzie, and the three girls headed to the marsh.

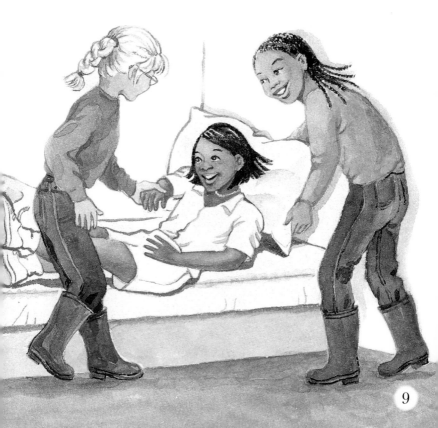

CHAPTER 2

Dead Fish

The girls walked toward the meadow. The ground started getting softer and wetter.

Murky water covered Robin's shoes. "The ground's all wet."

Nezzie laughed. "That why they call it 'wetlands.' Dad said all of this used to be part of the marsh. A long time ago, people drained the land to plant crops and build houses."

Robin could see puddles of water among the tall grasses. "It doesn't look like they drained it very well."

"Dr. Jack used to say this area was supposed to stay moist," Theresa said.

"What's so important about wet dirt?" asked Robin. "You couldn't grow anything here. The roots would rot."

"There's plenty of stuff growing here," retorted Nezzie. "Grass and reeds and cattails. These plants give marsh creatures a safe home."

"You can see the lake now. Look, Robin," said Theresa.

Robin gazed across the road at the crystal clear water that was Hominy Ridge Lake. A flock of birds was resting peacefully on the surface of the water.

Just then Smitty bounded across the road, barking. The birds rose in the air in a cloud of wings and noisy honks. "Bad Smitty," yelled Nezzie.

Robin watched as the birds disappeared over the woods. "They're absolutely beautiful," she marveled. "What are they?"

"Canada geese," said Nezzie. "My favorite." Carefully, the girls walked down the bank to the creek that led to the lake. Nezzie breathed in the rich, moist air. "I love the smell of the water," said Nezzie. "It makes me think of coming here with Dad."

"Hey, I found a fish," called Robin, looking at the water. "A dead fish."

Nezzie and Theresa hurried over. A small fish floated belly-up among the tall grasses.

"There's another one," said Theresa.

"This is weird," commented Nezzie. "I wonder what happened."

"What's the big deal?" asked Robin. "Fish die all the time."

"Sure," said Nezzie, "but not so many at once." She sniffed, wrinkling her nose like a cat. "Something smells funny. It's coming from the lake."

"This whole place smells," muttered Robin.

The girls followed the trail that led to the lake. Suddenly Nezzie came to a stop. "Oh, no!" she exclaimed. Ahead of the girls stretched a sandy beach. But it was anything but a pleasant sight. Dead fish were everywhere.

Robin covered her nose and mouth to keep out the awful smell. At last, she managed to gasp out some words. "What happened?"

"I don't know," said Nezzie. "Fish just don't die like this."

"Something must be wrong with the water," said Theresa. "I don't know what else could do this."

"Let's get out of here," said Robin. "These dead fish are giving me the creeps."

Ignoring her stepsister, Nezzie picked up a stick and stirred the water with it.

"Come on," urged Robin. "This place reeks. I think I'm going to be sick."

Robin stepped back a few paces, hoping to get away from the smell. She waited impatiently for the other girls.

A moment later, Nezzie appeared. "Look, I'm sorry. But this is important. Something bad happened."

Robin just nodded. Together, the girls returned to the beach to join Theresa.

"Did something get into the water?" asked Theresa.

"I don't know what else could cause this," said Nezzie.

"Maybe it's an oil spill," said Robin.

"I don't think so," said Theresa. "The water doesn't look oily."

She frowned in thought. "I think we should go home and call Uncle Bill," she said.

"Who's Uncle Bill?" asked Robin.

"He's an aquatic specialist," explained Nezzie. "He'll know what to do."

"Well, let's get out of here, then." Robin was more than willing to leave the dead fish—and the soggy marsh—to someone else.

CHAPTER 3

The Investigation Begins

The girls were breathless by the time they reached the Jones's house. "What's your hurry?" asked Mrs. Jones.

"We found a lot of dead fish, Mama. We need to call Uncle Bill right away," said Nezzie.

"You didn't touch anything, did you?"

"No, we just looked," Nezzie assured her.

"Well, go wash your hands anyway." Mrs. Jones said. "All of you. Then you can call Bill. I know he'll want to hear about this."

Two minutes later, Nezzie was dialing. Robin and Theresa stood quietly, listening.

"Mama, he wants us to meet him at the bridge so we can show him where the fish are," Nezzie said.

"Let me talk to him," Mrs. Jones said, taking the phone from her daughter.

Nezzie whispered to the others, "At first he just asked for directions. But I convinced him to let us come along."

"Why?" asked Robin. "Can't we just turn this over to him? We're supposed to be researching the food chain."

"This is research," said Nezzie. "Fish are part of the food chain. If something is wrong with the fish, something could be wrong with whatever eats them or whatever they are eating."

Mrs. Jones hung up. "All right, girls," she said. "You'd better get going. Bill's leaving right now."

Ten minutes later, the girls arrived at the bridge just as a truck pulled up. Nezzie and Theresa ran to the man who got out.

"How you girls doing?" the man asked. "You must be Robin," he said. "I'm Bill Harris. I met your dad a couple of weeks ago." He shook Robin's hand. "Those two call me Uncle Bill. I taught them all they know about fishing. You can call me Uncle Bill, too, if you like."

Robin felt instantly comfortable with him. "I'd like that, sir."

"No need to 'sir' me," he said. "OK, tell me what's happened."

The girls filled him in. He listened intently.

"All right. Get in the truck, and we'll drive down there," said Uncle Bill.

The girls climbed in the backseat. They bumped over the rough road to Hominy Ridge Lake. Once there, Uncle Bill lifted the tailgate and started removing supplies. He handed out gloves, saying, "Put these on."

The girls pulled on the gloves while Uncle Bill lifted a large box and a cooler from the truck. "We need to keep our specimens cold until we get them to the small biology lab in town," explained Uncle Bill.

He handed each girl a quart-size jar. "These are for taking water samples."

Robin watched as Uncle Bill took the lid off and swished it around in the water. He did the same thing with the jar. Next, he filled the jar with water and screwed the lid back on.

The girls copied his actions carefully. Then they followed Uncle Bill back up the bank. He took the lid off the cooler and put the jars inside so the ice surrounded them.

"Now we're going to collect some dead fish," said Uncle Bill. He eyed Robin's sneakers. "Since you aren't wearing boots, you'd better help me wrap fish, Robin."

Holding a net, he waded into the lake. He dipped the net beneath a floating fish to catch it. As he came back to the shore, he said, "Nezzie and Theresa, you can net more samples. Then bring them to Robin and me."

Uncle Bill ripped off a sheet of aluminum foil and wrapped it around the fish, which he handed to Robin. "You can pack our samples in the ice cooler."

Robin looked uneasily at the foil-wrapped fish. Yuck, she thought. Thank goodness for gloves!

They all worked steadily. "OK, girls," said Uncle Bill, "I think we've got enough."

As Uncle Bill started the engine, Robin stared out the window, thinking about dry shoes and clean clothes. She wasn't entirely sure how happy she was about being part of this detective team.

Uncle Bill pulled into the driveway at Goose Haven Farm. The girls jumped out of the truck. "As soon as I know something, I'll call you." Uncle Bill waved to everyone and drove off.

CHAPTER 4

A Mountain of Clues

"OK," said Mr. Jones, "while we eat lunch, you can tell us about this discovery you made in the marsh."

As they ate, the girls told their story. Mr. Jones said, "This whole thing worries me, especially since the creek is so close to the farm."

"I want to look around some more," said Nezzie. "Why don't we go back this afternoon?"

Later that afternoon, the girls retraced their steps to the lake. Mr. and Mrs. Jones walked behind them.

Long before they got to the water, the smell of dead fish reached them. "Whew!" said Mr. Jones. "It's pretty smelly."

At the beach, Mr. and Mrs. Jones studied the scene with horror. "Man," said Robin's father, "what a mess!"

"Mama, Papa Tom," called Nezzie, "we're going to follow the creek for a bit. We want to see if there's anything else up there."

"Go ahead," said Mrs. Jones. "We're right behind you." She picked her way along the path. "But if you find any other signs of trouble, you call us."

"OK," said Nezzie. They hadn't gone too far before Nezzie asked, "What's that? See where the creek curves around into those trees?"

Robin squinted. "You're right. There is something there."

"Come on," said Nezzie. The girls hurried along the creek bank.

Nezzie turned around and yelled, "Hey, Mama! Papa Tom! There's something up here."

Mr. and Mrs. Jones caught up with the girls. Robin could see the mound clearly now. "Yuck! It's garbage!"

A huge pile of trash started at the edge of a side road. It tumbled down into the creek.

"Where in the world did this come from?" asked Mrs. Jones.

"Somebody's been illegally dumping," said Mr. Jones.

"I wonder how long this garbage has been here," said Mrs. Jones.

"We were here just a month ago, Mama," said Nezzie. "We came out for a picnic."

"I remember," said her mother. "There was certainly no trash here then."

"So who dumped it?" asked Theresa. "And when did they do it?"

"And why?" added Robin. "Why would anyone do such a disgusting thing?"

"Since when did you care about the environment?" Nezzie asked Robin.

"Just because I don't like the marsh doesn't mean I don't care about nature," said Robin.

Theresa bent to pick something up.

"Don't touch anything!" said Mr. Jones.

"It's just a piece of paper," protested Theresa. "There's a name or something on it."

"No," said Mr. Jones, "Who knows what's in this mess. Come on. We're going home to call Uncle Bill."

CHAPTER 5

Camping Out

"What did he say?" asked Robin as soon as her father had hung up the phone.

"He was upset, but he wasn't surprised. He's going to notify the authorities," said her dad.

"There are plenty of landfills," said Robin. "Why don't they just go there?"

"Some people don't want to pay the fees that landfills charge," said Mrs. Jones. "Hopefully the authorities will put a stop to it."

The girls gathered upstairs in Nezzie's room. "I knew something got into the water," said Nezzie. "Now we know how."

"What I want to know is who put that stuff there," Robin said.

"What if we could catch someone in the act?" asked Theresa. "We could camp out and wait for someone to show up with a load of trash."

"I'll go ask Mama if we can camp," said Nezzie. Five minutes later, she was back. "Start packing," she said. "We're going camping."

"I'll be back in 15 minutes," promised Theresa.

By the time Nezzie and Robin dragged their things downstairs and onto the porch, Theresa was back.

Mr. and Mrs. Jones came out to say goodbye. "Do you have girls have everything?" asked Mrs. Jones.

"I don't know," said Robin. "It seems to me that we ought to need more than a flashlight, water, cookies, and fruit."

"If we need anything else, we're close enough to come back and get it," said Nezzie.

"I guess," said Robin. "I've never been camping before."

"You'll enjoy it." said Mrs. Jones. "The meadow is great. It's close enough to be safe, but far enough away so you'll feel like you're on your own."

"I'm not sure about letting them camp by themselves, Jill," said Mr. Jones.

"It's perfectly safe," said Mrs. Jones. "They'll be in our backyard." Robin looked at Nezzie. Wasn't the whole point of camping to watch the dump site? Could they see it from the meadow?

"We'll be fine, Papa Tom," Nezzie said.

"All right," he replied. "We'll see you in the morning."

As soon as they were out of hearing distance, Robin said, "I'm not sure about this. Dad thinks we're camping in the meadow. We're not, are we?"

"Camping near the dump site is the only way to see what's going on. If they knew where we were really going, they wouldn't let us," said Nezzie.

Robin didn't like misleading her father. But she certainly didn't want Nezzie to think she was afraid of camping near the dump site, even if she was.

"We can camp by that grove of trees where we found those arrowheads last summer," said Nezzie.

Theresa said, "We can use my binoculars to spy on the dump site."

By the time the sky began to darken, the tent was up, and they were in their sleeping bags.

CHAPTER 6

Plan B

The next thing Robin knew, the sun was up. "Hey, guys, wake up," she cried.

The girls stumbled out of the tent, stretching and yawning. A quick check with the binoculars revealed no sign of new dumping.

"A whole night wasted," said Nezzie wearily.

"Yeah," agreed Robin. "Let's go home and figure out what to do next."

The girls stowed the tent in the shed. "I wonder when Uncle Bill will know something," said Theresa.

"Not before Tuesday, that's for sure," said Robin.

"Right," said Nezzie, "so on to Plan B."

"Hey," said Theresa, "Maybe we could go back and find that letter I saw. It could give us a clue about who is doing the dumping."

"Maybe," Robin said. "The letter might have a name or address that tells us who the garbage belongs to. Then maybe we can find out who dumped it there."

"So let's all meet here after lunch," said Nezzie.

Robin and Nezzie had come up with Plan B while they dressed. Robin had held firm on one thing. "We have to tell Dad and Mama Jill what we're doing," she had insisted. "I don't want to spend the rest of my life grounded."

Nezzie had agreed. Now as the family was finishing breakfast she said, "Mama, we've been thinking about the marsh. We've been learning in school that we have to be caretakers of the environment. Whoever is doing the dumping is anything but a good caretaker."

"I agree with you there," said Mrs. Jones. "It's an awful thing to do."

"Robin and I were wanted to check out the dump site again," said Nezzie. "We thought that maybe we could figure out who's doing the dumping."

"Absolutely not!" said Mr. Jones. "Do you know how dangerous messing around with that trash could be?"

"Tom," said Mrs. Jones, "let's not be too quick to say no. Let me tell you some things, and then we can make a decision.

"A few years ago, there was a cleanup at Reservoir Park. The park had gotten really polluted. They asked for volunteers, and Jack and I took Nezzie and Theresa along with us. The whole event was carefully supervised and there were specific guidelines. I think if they just look around the edges of the dump site, it would be safe enough. We'll go with them again."

"What exactly are you girls looking for?" Mr. Jones asked.

"Theresa saw a letter," said Robin. "If we could find names or addresses, we'd have something to go on."

"The letter was right out in the open. We wouldn't have to dig through the trash. We could wear gloves," said Nezzie.

Robin touched her father's shoulder. "Dad, we just want to look around."

Mr. Jones hesitated. "OK," he said, "but you have to follow my instructions exactly."

"I assume that Theresa is in on this plan of yours, too," said Mrs. Jones.

"Of course," said Nezzie. "We'll call her as soon as we get home.

CHAPTER 7

In Search of Clues

That afternoon, the group descended upon the dump site. "Stay on the outer edges of the pile. No climbing. Do you understand me?" Mrs. Jones said.

"We remember everything you told us," said Robin. "Only pick up what you can see clearly. Use a shovel to dig in the muck. Change gloves every so often. Stay off the pile of trash."

Her father smiled. "Sounds like you know what to do. Let's get started."

Theresa immediately went to look for the envelope she had spied on the first trip. After a few minutes, she called out, "I found something!" She lifted a soggy sheet of paper.

"The writing is all smeared," said Robin. "Maybe after it dries out we can read it."

Theresa carried the paper over to Mrs. Jones.

"Our first piece of evidence," said Nezzie's mother. She spread the paper on top of a garbage bag she had put on the ground.

A few minutes later, Robin said, "There's a lot of mail here. This is addressed to Supreme Painters."

"That explains some of the stuff I'm finding," said Mr. Jones. "Paint cans. Half-empty bottles of paint remover."

"Tom, can you get those cans floating in the reeds over there?" Mrs. Jones pointed.

He scooped up the two containers and read the labels aloud. "Malathion." He shook his head. "This is bad, girls. Malathion is a poison."

"We'd better tell Uncle Bill," said Nezzie.

As soon as they got back to the house, Mr. Jones called Uncle Bill. Meanwhile, the girls laid out the papers, which were now dry.

"One of these letters has Pest Control at the top, but the first part of the name is gone," said Theresa. "There's a bug with a circle around it and a line through it."

"Let's try to look it up," suggested Nezzie. She hurried off, returning with a phone book. She flipped through it.

"Oh no," wailed Theresa, "look at all the different companies!"

They spent the next half hour thumbing through the phone book and writing down phone numbers.

"Most of the mail we found is from the same four businesses," Nezzie said.

"They must be dumping, don't you think?" asked Theresa.

Robin shook her head. "It wouldn't make sense for four different companies to be dumping their trash in the same spot at the same time. I'll bet these companies paid someone else to haul it away," said Robin.

Nezzie broke in. "If we can find who they hired to do their hauling, we'll know who dumped the trash."

"I know!" cried Theresa. "We could call the companies and say we were working on a school project about landfills and ask them if they handled their trash or if they hired somebody else to do it."

Mrs. Jones looked thoughtful. "Well, you are working on a school project. This all came out of that food chain assignment, so that much is true. I don't see any harm in contacting the businesses with the survey idea."

Mr. Jones said, "You're not calling any hauling companies. Whoever is doing the dumping is breaking the law and knows it. Bill's people can handle it from that point."

"Okay," said Robin, "Once we find out who the dumpers are, we'll tell you and Mama Jill."

"Don't forget, it's Sunday. Most places are closed," said Mrs. Jones. "You probably won't have any luck until Tuesday."

Even though they didn't want to admit it, the girls knew she was right. "What if those creeps decide to dump another load of garbage?" said Theresa.

"I think we should have another stakeout," whispered Nezzie. "Are you two in?"

"I'm in," said Theresa.

"Me, too," said Robin.

"Great," said Nezzie. "Now all we have to do is talk our parents into letting us camp out again tonight."

CHAPTER 8

More Detecting

"I hope they don't suspect anything," said Theresa.

"Well, we didn't lie," said Nezzie defensively. "We said we wanted to camp again. They didn't ask where."

"But you know they think we're in the meadow," commented Robin.

"Yeah," admitted Nezzie. "I don't feel good about this, Robin, but they wouldn't have given us permission to camp here."

"It's for a good cause," said Robin, "We're trying to catch the people spoiling our marsh."

"*Our* marsh," teased Nezzie. "Listen to you."

Robin grinned. "I admit it. I like the butterflies and the wildflowers. And that crane we saw this afternoon was gorgeous."

"Shhh! Did you hear something?" asked Nezzie suddenly. However, they heard nothing but the swish of grass blowing against the side of the tent.

Theresa looked over at Smitty, who was lying peacefully just outside the tent. "If there was something out there, Smitty would have let us know."

"I guess you're right," said Nezzie.

Once again, Robin struggled to keep her eyes open. The next thing she knew, light filled the tent. They had fallen asleep—again.

"Nezzie! Theresa!" called Robin. "Wake up!"

"Some detectives we are," Nezzie grumbled. "I can't believe we didn't stay awake."

A short time later, they were headed to the house. "We'll have to help Mama get things ready for the cookout. We've got lots of company coming," said Nezzie.

"I'll call you later," said Theresa. She took off down the road toward her own house.

The rest of the day passed quickly. Robin enjoyed every minute of the Labor Day celebration. She had never seen so much food!

Later on they played a game of touch football. After football, it was time for volleyball. And when that was done, it was time for dessert.

When the visitors left, Robin stood in the driveway and waved until her arm was tired. She'd had so much fun. By six o'clock, she and Nezzie were done helping with cleanup. They immediately started discussing the marsh.

"Too bad we still don't know about that pest control business. If we could find out who they are, it would be a good lead," Nezzie said.

"What about the Internet?" said Robin.

"Good idea!" said Nezzie, "Mama, may we use the computer for a while? We need to check something out on the Internet."

"Go ahead," said Mrs. Jones.

In the office, Robin punched a few keys on the keyboard. "Let's do a search for 'pest control' and 'Fort Wayne, Indiana.'" A selection of entries popped up.

They scrolled down the list. "We only need to check the ones that are businesses," said Robin. She clicked on a name. And another. Each time, the logos weren't right.

Twenty names later, Robin clicked on Duncan's Pest Control. "This is it!" she yelled. "Look!"

There on the screen was a big fat bug in a circle with a line through it.

CHAPTER 9

Grounded

"I thought school would never end," said Nezzie as the bus stopped at Goose Haven Farm. The girls raced to the phone to make their calls.

"Let's try Duncan's Pest Control," Nezzie suggested, dialing the number. "Hello? This is Inez Anderson. I'm working on a school science project about landfills. I just have two questions. Do you take care of your own waste removal or does someone do that for you?" Nezzie hastily scribbled down an answer. "Thank you," she said. "Do you know where they take your trash?" She scribbled some more. "Thank you."

Nezzie hung up. "She said Acme Hauling and Waste Removal takes their trash to the landfill."

"This is the best clue so far," said Theresa, dialing Supreme Painters. After she was finished with the call, she said, "It's Acme Hauling and Waste Removal again."

Next Nezzie called Windmere Roofing. Robin and Theresa listened as she asked the questions.

"Bingo!" cried Nezzie as she replaced the receiver. "Another contract with Acme!"

"Obviously, Acme is dumping the stuff in the marsh," said Robin.

"I think you're right," agreed Nezzie. "These businesses are all different. The only thing they have in common is that Acme hauls their trash."

"Let's tell Mama Jill and Dad what we've found out," suggested Robin. The girls went to find Mr. and Mrs. Jones.

"We think we know who's doing the illegal dumping," announced Nezzie. "Acme Hauling and Waste Removal."

"Are you sure?" said Mrs. Jones.

"We're sure, Mama," said Nezzie. She showed her mother the notes from their phone calls.

"I'll call Bill and let him know what you found out. Then he can get the authorities involved." Mr. Jones reached for the phone.

"What'd he say?" asked Robin after her dad made the call.

"He said that you were great detectives and he thought you had some good evidence against Acme Hauling."

"Yes!" yelled Robin and Nezzie.

"He'll stop by tomorrow to pick up your notes to turn them over to the authorities." Mr. Jones grinned. "They'll have the case solved in no time."

"But we wanted to catch them in the act. Like real detectives," said Robin.

Mrs. Jones chuckled. "So what would real detectives do?"

"Don't encourage them!" said Mr. Jones. "The next thing you know, they'll be wanting to stake out the site and catch the bad guys on tape."

"The video camera," said Theresa. "Why didn't we think of that the last time?"

"What last time?" said Mrs. Jones.

"Oops," said Theresa, covering her mouth.

Mrs. Jones looked sternly at Nezzie. "Inez Denise Anderson, tell me exactly what Theresa is talking about."

Suddenly, all three girls were talking at once. They tried to explain about the camping trips. That they knew they were supposed to stay in the meadow. That somehow they had gotten the idea about watching the dump site and ended up in the marsh.

Mr. Jones frowned. "I can't believe you girls! We trusted you!"

The girls hung their heads in shame.

"All three of you knew where we expected you to be. What if something had happened? No one would have been there to help you." Mrs. Jones glared at Nezzie and Robin. "The two of you are grounded until further notice." Then she glared at Theresa.

"And I'm calling your mother. Robin, Nezzie, upstairs. Theresa—you had better head home."

"You and your big mouth," muttered Nezzie as the three girls left the room.

"I'm sorry," said Theresa. "It sort of slipped out."

"Yeah, and now we're 'sort of' grounded," grumbled Robin.

CHAPTER 10

Unexpected Help

When they got home from school on Wednesday, Robin and Nezzie went straight to Mrs. Jones's office to use the computer. Their science report was due the next day.

"We've got to get the final report done tonight," said Robin.

"Too bad Theresa isn't here," commented Nezzie. "She has a lot of stuff we need."

"We could e-mail her," suggested Robin.

"OK," said Nezzie.

They got to work, looking over the information they had collected. "One thing I want in our report is how the food chain is balanced," said Nezzie. "I want to show that people's actions can mess it up."

"Yeah," said Robin. "I hadn't thought about that before. I just figured everything was the way it's supposed to be and it would stay that way."

Robin smiled at Nezzie. "I guess this project has made me look at things differently."

As soon as the girls finished going through their notes, they e-mailed Theresa.

The girls e-mailed back and forth for several hours. At last they were done.

"Wow, I can't believe we finished so quickly," said Nezzie. "You're a great writer, Robin.

"Let's have Mama take a look at this," Nezzie added. "I always have her read my reports before I turn them in."

The girls found Mrs. Jones in the kitchen. "Mama," said Nezzie, "would you look at this for us? It's our report on the food chain."

"Sure," she said. After she finished, she looked at the girls thoughtfully. "You three did a good job."

"Thanks, Mama Jill," said Robin.

"I'd like to see this again after you finish," said Mrs. Jones.

"Sure thing, Mama," said Nezzie. The girls hurried off to make the changes Mrs. Jones had suggested. By dinnertime, their final copy was ready to hand in. Nezzie took a second copy to her mother.

Later that night, Mr. Jones said, "We'd like to talk to you, girls. We read your report. We think that we should help you guys solve this mystery."

"What?!" exclaimed Nezzie.

"Don't get the wrong idea," said her mother. "You're still grounded as punishment for lying. However," she added, "after reading your report, we understand your dedication to clearing up this mystery."

"I'm also very happy to see how passionate you've become, Robin," said her father. "I can see that you've developed a real appreciation for the environment."

"Tom and I have decided to camp out with you so we can help you stake out the dump site," Mrs. Jones said. "I'll call Theresa's mother and ask if Theresa can join us on a stakeout tonight."

Nezzie threw her arms around her mother. "Thank you!"

"Let's take the video camera. That way we can catch them on tape," said Robin.

Her father shook his head. "Stakeouts. Video cameras. I can't believe I agreed to go along with this scheme."

Robin grinned. "Like it or not, you're becoming part of the detective team, Dad."

CHAPTER 11

Caught in the Act

"Everybody ready?" called Mr. Jones.

"Everyone except Smitty," said Nezzie. They had agreed to leave the dog at home, since his barking might alert the dumpers. The three girls led the way as the group headed into the marsh.

In a short time they reached the campsite. "We'll take turns keeping an eye on the dump site," said Robin's father. "We'll use my watch. It has an alarm we can set to signal the next shift."

During Robin's watch, she kept thinking about the dumpers. She wished she could meet them face-to-face and tell them exactly what she thought of them. How could they let poisons loose in the marsh? Didn't they care that they were killing marsh animals?

She was almost nodding off when the alarm sounded. She went to get her father, who had the next watch. Then she crawled into her sleeping bag.

It was daylight when Robin opened her eyes again.

"Nothing happened," said Nezzie glumly.

"That's okay," said Mr. Jones. "Our detective team will work until we solve this mystery."

We really are a team, thought Robin happily.

Half an hour later, they were home. "I'll take you to school," Mr. Jones said.

Robin, Nezzie, and Theresa rushed upstairs to shower and dress. They hurried outside to the car.

"Did you remember our report?" asked Theresa.

"I've got it," said Nezzie, patting her backpack.

"There's still the oral presentation," sighed Robin. "I'm dreading that."

"Come on, Robin," said Nezzie. "You'll do fine."

"Yeah," added Theresa. "This is the best report I've done. And it's because of you."

Robin looked at them. "Do you mean that?"

"Absolutely," said Nezzie. "You may not have liked the marsh at first, Robin, but you really got into it."

"Let's be sure we work together the next time we have to do a project," said Theresa.

A feeling of satisfaction washed over Robin. Even if she messed up on the oral presentation, she didn't care. Not if Nezzie and Theresa wanted her to work with them again. Not if they were her friends.

All morning, she watched the clock creep toward 1:00, when it was time for science class. At lunchtime, she could hardly eat. She sat at the table in science class, reading her notes over and over.

"Robin, you're next," said Mrs. Knox.

Robin got to her feet. She shuffled through her notes, her heart thumping wildly. Then she looked at Nezzie and Theresa. They both winked at her.

Robin stuck her notes into her pocket and started to talk. At first her voice quavered, but it soon got stronger.

"When we got this assignment," she said, "I didn't want to study the marsh. I thought it was dirty and slimy. But now I know better. It's a carefully balanced ecological system. We can upset that balance if we're not careful. It's up to every one of us to make sure that doesn't happen. We're all responsible for keeping the environment clean. That's what I got from this project. And that's what I'm going to remember from now on."

She sat down before her legs collapsed under her. Nezzie gave her a thumbs up.

That night, Robin had the third watch of the stakeout. She was half-dozing when she heard the low drone of a truck engine. The sound got louder and louder.

"Someone's coming!" she hissed. "Wake up, you guys!" Shivering with excitement, she looked through the binoculars. She could just make out a dump truck.

"What is it?" whispered her father.

Robin handed him the binoculars. "Look at the edge of the road," she said. "There's a dump truck there. It's Acme, I'm sure."

"Well, let's get our evidence," Mr. Jones said. Robin's hands shook slightly as she lifted the camera. Through the lens, she followed the truck down the road.

She taped the trash rolling out of the truck and onto the heap at the edge of the water. The black lettering of Acme Hauling and Refuse Removal stood out against the white background of the truck. She kept on taping until the dumping was finished. "We've got them!" said Robin as she turned off the camera.

CHAPTER 12

In the News

"We should've heard something by now," said Nezzie. "It's been two whole weeks."

"Dad said these things take time," said Robin. She picked up the remote control and turned on the television. "It feels so good not to be grounded. I never knew I'd miss the telephone and television so much."

Suddenly Nezzie let out an excited yelp. "Robin! Go back to Channel 25!"

There on the television screen was an Acme dump truck.

"It's our tape," gasped Theresa.

A voiceover said, "What you see here is actual footage of the illegal dumping that's been going on at Marin Marsh. Acme Hauling and Refuse Removal has been indicted on several counts of environmental pollution."

"They've been caught!" shouted Robin.

The voiceover continued, "Three local girls are credited with alerting the Department of Natural Resources to the illegal dumping. This is a copy of the videotape they made by going undercover."

"Undercover!" hollered Nezzie. "We're real detectives!"

The television showed a reporter standing on the beach at Hominy Ridge Lake. The reporter explained, "Some of the refuse that was dumped into the marsh contained a pesticide called malathion, which was deadly to these fish. Sadly, it will take some time to get the water back to normal."

Robin jumped to her feet. "We got them!"

The next day, the indictment of Acme Hauling was front-page news in the Fort Wayne News Journal.

Robin read every word of the article. "It says that if Acme is convicted, they have to pay for the cleanup, and they'll get fined, and some company officials could even go to jail," she reported.

"Yeah, and that's not all," said Nezzie, who was looking through another section of the paper. "Listen to this!" She started to read:

"Three students from Louis Middle School, Inez Anderson, Robin Jones, and Theresa Meyers, were instrumental in breaking up the illegal dumping operation. 'The city of Fort Wayne is fortunate to have such responsible young people living in our community,' said Mayor Worth. 'I will be contacting them and their parents to issue an invitation to next month's Community Service Awards banquet. They have earned this honor for their dedication to the environment.'"

"An award!" shouted Nezzie. "This is even better than the *A* we got on our project!"

Robin looked from Nezzie's beaming face to Mama Jill's wide grin to her father's proud smile. "An award is pretty cool," she agreed, "but getting to be part of an awesome family of detectives is even better." The smiles got even bigger. Robin's was the biggest of all.